# THE OFFICIAL

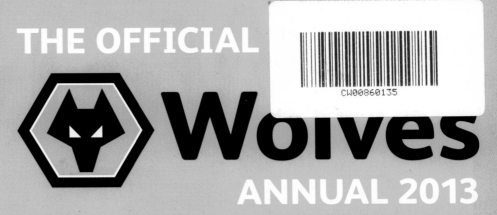

# Wolves
## ANNUAL 2013

CW00860135

**Written by Paul Berry**

**Designed by Mathew Whittles**

A Grange Publication

© 2012. Published by Grange Communications Ltd., Edinburgh, under licence from Wolverhampton Wanderers Football Club. Printed in the EU.

Every effort has been made to ensure the accuracy of information within this publication but the publishers cannot be held responsible for any errors or omissions. Views expressed are those of the author and do not necessarily represent those of the publishers or the football club. All rights reserved.

Photographs © AMA Sport Photo Agency, Sam Bagnall, Dave Bagnall.

Additional Photography: SM2 Studio, Les Hurley, Man Utd Pics, www.daredevil-creative.com.

With thanks to Synaxis Design Consultancy, Sky Sports.

ISBN no. 978-1-908925-18-3

£7.99

# Contents

# STÅLE CHECKS IN!

Ståle Solbakken may be the first overseas manager to take the helm at Molineux.

But his arrival back in May of 2012 certainly wasn't the first contact he had enjoyed with the good ship Wolverhampton Wanderers!

No. Solbakken's first experience of Wolves came as a young boy back in Norway, when the men in gold and black were on an end-of-season tour.

"I remember I was about ten I think and Wolves came over to the little village where I was living," he recalls.

"There were some legends in the team like Steve Kindon, Kenny Hibbitt, Willie Carr and Derek Parkin.

"That was my first meeting with the Wolves shirt – and they beat our local team 6-0!"

All at Wolves are hoping that will prove something of a

good omen for the man who headed into the 2012/13 Championship season at Molineux with plenty of high-level experience under his belt – as both player and manager.

A midfielder by trade, Solbakken won 58 caps for Norway, scoring nine goals, and appeared at the 1998 World Cup and 2000 European Championships.

Title-winning medals in Denmark with both Aalborg and Copenhagen were among the honours achieved as a player, and he was named Norwegian Midfielder of the Year in 1995.

A heart attack suffered whilst training – from which he fully recovered – eventually finished Solbakken's career in 2001, but not without having enjoyed six months

in the Premier League with Wimbledon several years earlier.

"I remember the manager Joe Kinnear used to shout a lot," he recalls with a smile.

"One day I shouted back - and that was the end of me at Wimbledon!"

Solbakken has admitted to the odd moment of temper – a few YouTube clips including one with then Barcelona manager Pep Guardiola bear testimony to that – but is usually a far more measured and engaging personality with a fierce ambition, all qualities which helped land him the role back in May.

That ambition is also stirred by the fact that – like Wolves – Solbakken endured a massively disappointing 2011/12 campaign, an ultimately short-lived spell with FC Köln in the Bundesliga ending with relegation and his dismissal in April.

"It's fair to say that, like Wolves, I am looking for 'revenge' this season," he says.

Before that however, Solbakken's managerial CV stands up to the utmost scrutiny.

An early promotion with former club Ham Kam was merely the starter for a main course at Copenhagen which was to include five league titles and a Danish Cup triumph in 2009 heralding a league and cup double.

Not only that but Solbakken led Copenhagen into the group stages of the 2006/07 Champions League and, while eliminated at that stage, results included a 1-0 win over Manchester United.

Even better was to follow in the 2010/2011 season, when Copenhagen became the first team from Denmark to reach the last 16 of the Champions League, where they were beaten by Chelsea over two legs. In the group stages they had also held Barcelona to a 1-1 draw.

Solbakken was also named Danish Manager of the Year in both 2007 and 2011.

What then is the secret of the Solbakken success thus far? Difficult for him to say of course, but he is keen to continue his strength of man-management, believing his own experiences as a player can help.

"I've been a player myself – I know what players think and I've got a pretty good view of painting a picture on the training ground so players can understand what they're supposed to do in a game.

"I like to be out on the training pitch every day, sometimes coaching, sometimes observing, and I like to know the players I work with a little bit as people as well.

"I like to have them close to me but also have the professional distance that you want between a manager and the players.

"I like to feel I know them a little bit because then I can get the last five to ten per cent out of them.

"And when I build a team around me I also like people to take responsibility.

"It's not me sitting there thinking I know everything.

"When you have guys around you that have competence I think it's important to use that."

That applies to highly-rated first team coach Johan Lange, whom Solbakken brought in at the start of pre-season having worked with him back at Copenhagen.

Lange has been very much the eyes and ears for Solbakken, working not only on the training ground but also in scouting players and opposition teams.

With the DVD's of last season watched and digested, on top of the extensive knowledge of English football enjoyed by many in Scandinavia, the new manager headed into the new campaign with relish and excitement, backed up by a string of new signings including Tongo Doumbia, Slawomir Peszko, Georg Margreitter and Razak Boukari.

"I always thought it would be very intense and very close and I go into it under no illusions," he says.

"I can't promise anything but I know expectations are high for the team to do well.

"We will try everything we can to keep the supporters happy and if we do that then I think we will have a good season.

"I'm looking forward to the challenges here and I think the fans have reasons to be optimistic."

# BJORN AGAIN!

Björn – as in new Wolves striker Sigurdarson – is another word for 'Bear' in Icelandic.

But it was a 'Bull' for whom the summer arrival quickly learned about when checking in at Molineux in July.

Any aspiring, young striker who arrives at Wolves these days is probably never going to escape the comparison with the legend and record goalscorer by the name of Stephen George Bull.

But 21-year-old Sigurdarson takes it all in good grace!

"I was told a lot about Steve Bull when I joined," he says.

"Do I want to be like him? If that means scoring over 300 goals then yes of course!"

Sigurdarson headed into the new campaign boasting plenty of potential but well aware of the job on his hands in transferring his goalscoring abilities from the Norwegian Premier League and Lillestrom to the hustle and bustle of the Championship.

Comparisons with Bull don't exactly reduce any expectation levels from supporters, but the affable Icelander is confident he can handle the pressure of playing in English football's second tier.

"It does put pressure on me but I am ok with it," he says.

"It is good for the fans to have expectations of me and I will do my best to match them. And I will be ready for the physical challenge.

"I am fairly strong but I was working to be even stronger for the start of the season with my own individual programme when I arrived."

The boss Ståle Solbakken, who himself represented Lillestrom in his own playing days, was delighted to have captured the pacey and ambitious striker.

"I think it is a win-win situation for us," said Solbakken. His goalscoring ability can improve, his coolness can improve, but I can see the raw material is very much there.

"He's got the physique to handle the Championship, he's got speed, two good feet, and he can also jump well in the air. So if we can work with him each day and improve his understanding, he's got everything it takes to play at a higher level than now (Norway) and maybe higher than the Championship."

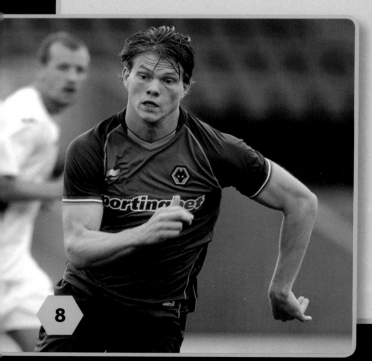

# LET'S ALL DO THE TONGO!

Time will tell, but it's usually never a bad sign for a player to have the crowd singing his name on his very first runout.

So it was in Tongo Doumbia's first Wolves appearance, in the pre-season friendly at Shrewsbury, that the travelling fans used a bit of footballing licence to sing "Let's all do the Tongo!" in deference to the Mali international.

The group of fans who accompanied the song with the conga were situated behind the goal into which Doumbia had just despatched his first goal in Wolves colours, a searing drive into the top corner after brushing aside a couple of challenges.

Coupled with a generally impressive 45 minutes either side of the goal, Doumbia's first impressions had his manager – as well as the Wolves fans – hoping for more to come!

"It may be dangerous to say it so early but I don't think we have done wrong with getting Doumbia," said Ståle Solbakken.

"I think he can do it for us, and he can cope with the English game because he is a natural born runner and athlete.

"When we were aware of him we quickly saw a lot of DVD's of him and I quickly rang a Norwegian player at Rennes (Alexander Tettey).

"He is young and has ability and last season was his breakthrough."

It was a one-year loan deal from Rennes with a view to a permanent deal which saw Doumbia join Wolves, with learning English one of the other tasks on the agenda!

"I am really looking forward to playing for the fans and the manager," he said via a translator.

"I want to help the team as much as I can as we aim for promotion.

"There were other clubs interested I had a good feeling about Wolves as soon as I spoke to the manager.

"I am also a strong player and like to battle as well and will give everything I have for the Wolves shirt and for the club."

# ◆ AUGUST

There was plenty of optimism at Molineux as Wolves headed into the 2011/12 season boosted by the arrival of three permanent signings.

Jamie O'Hara's loan spell at Tottenham progressed into a five year contract, Carling Cup winner Roger Johnson arrived from Birmingham to become captain, and keeper Dorus De Vries – who had kept a record number of clean sheets in helping Swansea to play-off success – checked in following the departure of Marcus Hahnemann.

A pre-season training camp in Ireland launched preparations while Wolves rounded off their friendly schedule on a high with successive victories against Celtic, Ipswich and Real Zaragoza.

And all that optimism proved justified in the season's opening salvos as Wolves kicked off the Barclays Premier League campaign with an unbeaten August.

The Blackburn bogey was laid to rest on the opening day as Steven Fletcher's header quickly cancelled out Marco Formica's strike and Stephen Ward pounced to lash home the

winner – and spare Kevin Doyle's blushes – after his fellow Irishman had missed a penalty.

That was the first Premier League win against Rovers in seven attempts, and provided the platform to also get the home programme off to a winning start against Fulham eight days later.

Doyle and Matt Jarvis were on target in a devastating three minute spell just before half time in the only fixture to be played in front of an empty North Bank end of the ground as the new lower tier of the stand neared completion.

The two successive wins were then followed by a hard-fought goalless draw away at Aston Villa, the lunchtime kick off ensuring that Wolves actually hit the heady heights of the Premier League's top spot for a short period after full time.

The general feelgood factor around Molineux had also been enhanced when 11 changes for the Carling Cup curtain-raiser at Northampton still resulted in a 4-0 win, Sylvan Ebanks-Blake (2), Nenad Milijaš and Sam Vokes the men on target.

There was one piece of sad news during the first month of the season however, when Wolves and Scotland legend Frank Munro passed away at the age of 63.

# ◆SEPTEMBER

If August was to provide a superb start to the new Barclays Premier League season then the wheel was to turn full circle in September.

Boss Mick McCarthy and the players had gone to great lengths to play down Wolves' impressive opening to the campaign given the unforgiving nature of life in the top flight.

And unfortunately they were to be proved right in a difficult month when Wolves lost all three of their fixtures in the league.

The visit of Tottenham Hotspur provided the first opportunity for supporters to sit in the new lower tier of the redeveloped Stan Cullis Stand.

Sadly there wasn't much for them to get excited about as a Spurs side, which had lost its first two games against Manchester United and Manchester City, struck twice in the last 23 minutes through Emmanuel Adebayor and Jermain Defoe to take the points.

Next up came an even more disappointing Molineux afternoon given it was against a team Wolves would expect to be battling alongside for league position during the season – newly-promoted Queens Park Rangers.

An awful start to the game saw Wolves 2-0 adrift after ten minutes, with a late goal from DJ Campbell ultimately handing the Londoners an even more comfortable margin of victory.

The final weekend of the month did provide a better performance if not result as Wolves travelled to face Liverpool at Anfield.

A controversial opener for the Reds after Roger Johnson appeared to be fouled was followed up by an impressive Luis Suarez effort, but a response from boyhood Liverpool fan Steven Fletcher shortly after half time gave the travelling fans' hope.

However despite spells of strong Wolves pressure in the second period, it wasn't to be as the Molineux Men suffered a third successive league defeat.

The silver lining to the September cloud had reared its head between the QPR and Liverpool games with a 5-0 Carling Cup thrashing of Millwall which included spectacular goals from Adam Hammill and Adlene Guedioura.

# ◆ OCTOBER

Life for Wolves didn't get much better in October either, with the early season form quickly becoming a fading memory as the winless streak continued.

Fixtures at home to Newcastle and away at West Bromwich Albion brought about the fourth and fifth successive league defeats although there were mitigating factors in both games to suggest things could have been different.

On a frustrating Molineux afternoon when Newcastle keeper Tim Krul was by far and away the man of the match, Wolves also counted the cost of a pair of hugely controversial decisions from the officials.

Already 2-0 down, a chance to get back into the game shortly before half time was missed when only a free kick was awarded for a challenge from Steven Taylor on Jamie O'Hara which was clearly inside the penalty area.

And then, with Wolves piling forward in injury time after Steven Fletcher's 88th minute goal, the assistant referee flagged that the ball had gone out of play before Matt Jarvis headed back for Kevin Doyle to scramble over the line.

Defeat in the Black Country derby at The Hawthorns was more self-inflicted, the team unable to take advantage of a greater share of possession and a golden early chance for Doyle to fall victim to a goal in each half from Chris Brunt and Peter Odemwingie.

Despite going 2-0 down for the sixth successive league fixture against Swansea, there were at least signs of the famed Molineux spirit as goals from Doyle and O'Hara inside the last six minutes secured a morale-boosting draw.

There was little chance to build on those small shoots of recovery however, as the month finished with successive defeats against in-form leaders Manchester City, 5-2 in the Carling Cup at Molineux and 3-1 in the league at the Etihad Stadium.

A welcome diversion from the season's troubles was provided by Matt Murray's testimonial in October, as stars from the world of football and showbiz – including a playing return for Mick McCarthy – entertained a crowd of almost 8,000 on a heartwarming Sunday afternoon at Molineux.

# ◆ NOVEMBER

The first fixture of November with Wigan heralded Wolves' Official Armed Forces Day at Molineux, including a series of events to mark Armistice Day and raise funds for Help For Heroes and the Mercian Regiment Benovelent Fund.

The specially designed shirts embroidered with a poppy were also auctioned off after the game to raise money for the Royal British Legion's annual appeal.

On the pitch there was the desperate need of a win after taking just one point from the previous seven games, not least as Wigan arrived at Molineux both three points and three places below Wolves, and occupying bottom spot in the table.

And that much-needed win was duly delivered, Wolves overcoming some nervous moments after Ben Watson cancelled out Jamie O'Hara's opener to emerge with a 3-1 victory thanks to second half strikes from Dave Edwards and Stephen Ward.

The international break therefore arrived at a time when Wolves had stopped the rot and were occupying a lofty 13th place in the table, but hopes of further improvement after the restart were once again affected by some controversial refereeing.

Wolves were coping well with the always tough test posed by Everton at Goodison Park, and were destined for a point with seven minutes remaining after Phil Jagielka's first half reply to Stephen Hunt's penalty.

But when Louis Saha tumbled under minimal contact from Ward, referee Jonathan Moss pointed to the spot, giving Leighton Baines the chance to blast home what proved to be the winner.

Things were always unlikely to get better as the month was completed with a trip to face Chelsea at Stamford Bridge, particularly as Wolves were 3-0 behind at the break, but they did rally to prevent any additional second half damage on an afternoon when substitute Anthony Forde made his first team debut.

On the country rather than club front, Wolves' Irish contingent were delighted to book their place at the summer's European Championships with a comfortable two-leg success against Estonia, Ward on target in the return leg at the Aviva Stadium as Dublin partied to celebrate qualification.

# ● DECEMBER

The sad passing of Wales manager Gary Speed was marked at the first game of December against Sunderland with Welsh internationals Wayne Hennessey, Dave Edwards and David Vaughan laying a wreath in the centre circle prior to a minute's applause.

The game itself featured a dramatic ending with the visitors going in front through Kieran Richardson and then squandering a great opportunity to go further ahead when Jody Craddock was harshly adjudged to have felled Sebastian Larsson.

Justice prevailed as Wayne Hennessey saved Larsson's penalty, and within 25 seconds Steven Fletcher had headed Wolves level, then popping up with a clinical winner with nine minutes remaining.

As with the Wigan victory the previous month, three points took Wolves clear of their opponents and this time up to 15th in the table, but successive defeats against Manchester United and Stoke swiftly changed the equation once again.

Fletcher again showed his liking for the big occasion by scoring at Old Trafford but Wolves were comfortably beaten 4-1, while yet another controversial decision – failure to send off Stoke's Jonathan Woodgate – didn't help in the home defeat against the Potters.

Wolves finished off the month and indeed the year 2011 with three successive draws, in extremely different circumstances.

First up came up a topsy turvy Tuesday night against Norwich, Wolves twice coming from behind to draw 2-2, and then – yet another – controversy against Arsenal at the Emirates.

That man Fletcher had found the net again with an instinctive header to cancel our Gervinho's Gunners opener, and Wolves were looking comfortable until the 75th minute incident when Stuart Attwell sent off Nenad Milijaš for a ball-winning challenge on Mikel Arteta.

Wolves managed to cling on for a point thanks to the excellence of Hennessey, but while the decision was roundly lambasted in footballing circles, the appeal lodged with the FA failed, prompting Mick McCarthy to turn his next press conference into a Film Club to discuss the issue with journalists.

After all that drama the final game of the year at relegation rivals Bolton was fairly tame by comparison, in-form Fletcher again on target in a 1-1 draw at the Reebok Stadium.

# ◆ JANUARY

Wolves headed into the New Year with two fresh additions to the squad – loan midfielder Emmanuel Frimpong from Arsenal and permanent signing, the versatile Eggert Jonsson from Hearts.

And top Gunner Frimpong was no doubt feeling very much at home given his first two appearances were against London opposition – Chelsea at home and Tottenham away.

Wolves put up a good fight against Chelsea, and when Stephen Ward cancelled out Ramires' opener with just six minutes remaining it looked like a point was on the cards.

But then up popped Frank Lampard, fortunate to be on the pitch after referee Peter Walton took a lenient approach to a reckless first half challenge on Adam Hammill, to knock home a cruel winner with just a minute of normal time remaining.

Wolves did however manage to come away with a 1-1 draw against in-form Spurs at White Hart Lane, Luca Modric equalising Steven Fletcher's predatory finish but the visitors staying firm to snare an excellent point.

There was a sense of renewed confidence about Wolves with the Frimpong/Karl Henry/Jamie O'Hara midfield triumvirate working well, and with the impressive Michael Kightly flying again after returning from a loan spell at Watford, the first half performance at home to Aston Villa was arguably the best of the season.

But then Frimpong got injured, and Henry sent off, and Villa overturned a 2-1 deficit to win 3-2 thanks to a Robbie Keane thunderbolt leaving Wolves with nothing to show for all their flowing first half football.

And the hangover to that disappointment appeared to emerge instantly, as the team slumped to a 3-0 defeat at home to Liverpool on the final day of the month, all the goals coming in the second half.

There was however some consolation after full time with the news that Spurs defender Sebastien Bassong had agreed to move to Molineux on loan until the end of the season.

January meanwhile saw Wolves exit the FA Cup, a goalless draw away at Birmingham followed by a 1-0 defeat in the replay with Wade Elliott grabbing the only goal.

There was some sad news off the pitch during the month with the death of long-serving former Wolves kitman Dave Plant, who passed away at the age of 72.

# ◆ FEBRUARY

There was little sign of what was to follow as February began with a vital victory at Queens Park Rangers.

On a day when snow swamped much of Britain – making for an uncomfortable journey home – fans edging their way back up the M40 were at least buoyed by a first away league win since the opening day of the season.

Loftus Road also provided a rare afternoon when Wolves finished up on the right end of a refereeing decision, albeit a correct one, as Djibril Cisse saw red for grabbing Roger Johnson by the face.

Rangers were into a 1-0 lead by that point thanks to Bobby Zamora, but the half time addition of Kevin Doyle to the Wolves ranks proved decisive, the Irishman immediately setting up Matt Jarvis for an equaliser before tucking home the winner himself on 71 minutes.

On the back of similar afternoons against Wigan and Sunderland, Wolves had once again managed to see off one of their nearby rivals at the time and victory took them out of the bottom three and level on points with QPR.

But unfortunately the relegation zone was a renewed foe once again after the next fixture – a desperately disappointing Black Country Derby with West Bromwich Albion.

Fans from both teams had joined forces for a 'March to Molineux' event walking from the Hawthorns prior to kick off which raised thousands of pounds for the Acorns charity and culminated in Kieren Caldwell (Albion) and Ian Marrey (Wolves) delivering the matchball to the centre circle before kick off.

On the pitch though there was only one team in it, Steven Fletcher's first half equaliser proving scant consolation as the Baggies ran out 5-1 winners.

The result also brought about the end of Mick McCarthy's near six-year tenure at Molineux as the manager was relieved of his duties the following morning.

On leaving the club McCarthy reflected on enjoying "the best of times" in the Wolves hotseat, thanking everyone concerned for their efforts in what had proved one of the most successful eras in modern times.

After an 11-day search to find McCarthy's replacement, the Wolves Board – having noted the players' responding well to assistant manager Terry Connor's leadership – announced that he would have the job for the final 13 games of the season.

And Connor's reign got off to an impressive start as Wolves came from 2-0 down at Champions League qualification-chasing Newcastle to secure a 2-2 draw thanks to second half goals from Jarvis and Doyle.

# ◆ MARCH

March was to prove a difficult month for Wolves with a mixture of heavy defeats against Fulham and Manchester United and hard-fought reverses against Blackburn, Norwich and Bolton.

The month got off to the worst possible start at Craven Cottage as a grey and wet day was matched by the performance as Wolves failed to deal with the early loss of the injured Karl Henry and finished up on the wrong end of a 5-0 scoreline.

The following weekend's visit of fellow strugglers Blackburn therefore took on monumental proportions, with Terry Connor handing a first Premier League start to young midfielder David Davis having recalled him from a loan spell with Chesterfield.

Davis's display was to prove a rare bright spot on another disappointing afternoon as a brace from the lively Junior Hoilett gave Rovers a 2-0 victory which left Wolves perched precariously above Wigan in bottom spot.

Morale had been lifted again by the following Sunday as title-chasing Manchester United checked in, the game preceded by a spell of applause for Bolton's Fabrice Muamba at the start of a long recovery process having suffered a cardiac arrest the day before.

Wolves were living with United until conceding from a set piece after 21 minutes, but the dismissal of Ronald Zubar for two yellow cards shortly before the break made an unlikely task nigh on impossible.

And so it was that United turned on the afterburners to improve their goal difference and run out comfortable 5-0 winners.

The team's character however remained intact, and they took the lead against Norwich at Carrow Road the following weekend through the in-form Matt Jarvis.

But unfortunately Norwich hit back to score twice through Grant Holt on an afternoon where another Wolves Academy graduate Johnny Gorman came off the bench for his debut.

Bolton on the final weekend of the month was very close to a mirror image of the home game with Aston Villa the previous month, particularly with the result – another 3-2 Molineux defeat.

Wolves had dominated for long periods, and again led through Kightly, but were unable to keep Bolton out at the other end and Jarvis's impressive late strike proved merely a consolation.

The game with Bolton had also been a landmark occasion for many Wolves supporters, with the popular A Load of Bull fanzine selling its final edition after 23 years, going out with a fabulous gesture of donating outstanding subscriptions to Wolves Community Trust.

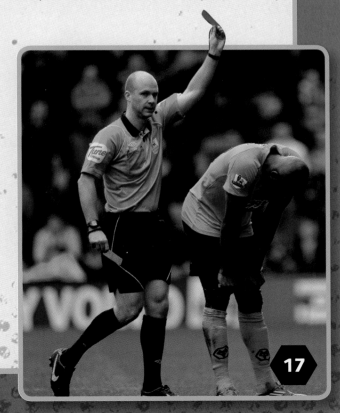

# ⬡ APRIL

Wolves went into April six points adrift at the foot of the Barclays Premier League table, but results elsewhere provided an opportunity to try and narrow that gap at a Saturday evening fixture at Stoke.

Things were looking good when Michael Kightly's attempted through ball found its way into the net to give Wolves the lead, but Robert Huth equalised and then Peter Crouch scored his second winner in the fixture during the season to seal victory for the Potters.

Wolves also finished up empty handed in their next fixture, at home to Arsenal, the game effectively over as a contest after Sebastien Bassong's early sending-off which pre-empted the Gunners running out 3-0 victors.

By this time relegation was looking inevitable, but Wolves were determined to go down fighting, battling to a 0-0 draw at Sunderland.

Yet in keeping with some of the fortune suffered during the season, keeper Wayne Hennessey's delight at a first clean sheet since August was quickly overshadowed by news he had torn his cruciate ligament and would be sidelined for an estimated six months.

So it was that Hennessey was missing and Dorus De Vries handed his Premier League debut for the next game, at home to eventual champions Manchester City.

This was the afternoon when relegation was sadly confirmed as Sergio Aguero and Samir Nasri gave City a 2-0 win, but there was inspiration from the Wolves fans who greeted the drop – and indeed a full time downpour – by cranking up the noise levels to show their support.

And the equally excellent away support enjoyed their day in Swansea on the final weekend of the month, even though it wouldn't have looked like it when Wolves were 3-0 down after 14 minutes and 4-1 down after 31.

Relegation may have been assured, but the squad weren't for lying down, and a superb comeback saw them hit back to draw 4-4 and indeed almost win the game through Kightly in the closing stages.

Elsewhere it was a superb month for the Wolves Women team, who followed up their Midland Combination League title success and promotion by making it a double with the League Cup as well. The Wolves ladies crowned a fabulous season by beating Stoke 2-0 in the final.

# ◆ MAY

Wolves rounded off a hugely disappointing home campaign at Molineux by welcoming Everton on the penultimate weekend of the season.

And despite another battling display, the players were unable to produce the win they were desperate for to reward both the loyal fans who had stuck with the team and the manager Terry Connor.

They did however add another point to their tally against an Everton side which extended their unbeaten run to nine with the goalless draw.

The club's End of Season awards winner took place in the following midweek, and was an understandably more low-key affair in comparison to previous seasons.

Wayne Hennessey took the Supporters' Player of the Year award with Steven Fletcher collecting the Players' Player accolade. Adlene Guedioura's strike against Millwall was voted Goal of the Season.

There was also even bigger news ahead of the final day trip to Wigan as the club confirmed the arrival of new manager, the Norwegian Ståle Solbakken.

The former international midfielder and manager of Copenhagen and Cologne agreed a deal to become manager from July 1 and was officially introduced to the press the day after the final fixture.

And despite all the trials and tribulations of such a difficult season, the Wolves fans who travelled to Wigan helped make it a carnival atmosphere as the squad bid farewell to the Premier League with a 3-2 defeat.

There were plenty of fancy dress costumes on show, not to mention a few songs of support for the soon-to-be-manager Solbakken.

But plenty of cheers were also reserved for Connor and the squad as they returned to the pitch to show their appreciation to the travelling support, having done the same to the home fans at Molineux after the game with Everton seven days earlier.

# MATCHDAY WORDSEARCH

The grid below contains various sights that you may well see in and around Molineux when you come and watch Wolves play. Can you find all of the items listed below? Either forwards, backwards or diagonally!

| B | N | N | U | T | S | O | P | L | A | O | G | O | L | A |
| W | A | I | Y | U | S | U | B | S | T | I | T | U | T | E |
| O | P | L | E | R | C | C | G | O | C | A | L | P | O | R |
| L | L | I | L | B | A | D | A | T | O | C | S | A | M | E |
| F | E | A | L | W | R | E | F | E | R | E | E | L | A | F |
| Q | N | M | O | A | F | C | O | R | N | E | F | E | N | F |
| R | N | Z | W | H | I | S | T | L | E | E | F | X | A | W |
| O | U | E | C | A | R | I | V | A | R | S | T | A | G | H |
| S | T | J | A | C | K | F | W | B | F | M | T | K | E | I |
| S | T | W | R | L | A | E | I | F | L | O | W | A | R | T |
| I | J | A | D | O | T | O | C | S | A | R | C | T | N | S |
| T | U | R | N | S | T | I | L | E | G | B | U | S | D | D |

BALL
CORNER FLAG
GOALPOST
MANAGER
MASCOT
REFEREE
SCARF
STAND
STEWARD
SUBSTITUTE
TURNSTILE
TUNNEL
WHISTLE
WOLFIE
YELLOW CARD

# OLD HABITS DIE HARD!

We asked the players what is their worst habit! Can you match the players on the list below with the habit?!

George Elokobi
Richard Stearman
Karl Henry
Sylvan Ebanks-Blake
Dave Edwards
Stephen Ward
Dorus De Vries
Stephen Hunt
Kevin Foley
Adam Hammill

**1** I moan more than most and I'm definitely not a morning person.

**2** Leaving dirty washing all over the house.

**3** I switch off very easily and have selective hearing.

**6** Slicing my drive when I play golf.

**7** I have none – I'm like Mary Poppins – perfect in every way.

**5** I'm a bit too energetic and noisy first thing in the morning.

**4** I turn the music right up in my car in the mornings – it helps wake me up!

**8** I 'click' the big toe on my left foot and can't go to sleep until I've found the right 'click'.

**9** I tend to get things off my chest and say things when other people would hold back.

**10** I always leave the dishes on the table instead of taking them to the kitchen.

Answers on Page 61

# THE SKY'S THE LIMIT

Sky's Soccer Saturday programme with Jeff Stelling has become the staple diet of many football fans for either the big match previews or – if they are unable to get along to a game – following the thrills and spills of the afternoon's fixtures from the comfort of their armchair.

But what's it like for the reporters who work on the show, whether compiling those previews or being despatched to a ground across the country to provide regular updates sometimes from slap, bang in the middle of a section of supporters?

Johnny Phillips is one of Soccer Saturday's most experienced reporters and, on top of that, is also a Wolves supporter, albeit one who has to remain objective when covering his team!

The Wolves Annual caught up with Johnny to find out more!

**So Johnny, how did you first get involved with journalism?**
I was hoping initially for a career in print journalism so I studied for a degree at Leeds University. While I was there I did a work placement with a press agency – I think they needed some cheap labour! – so I spent my last year of university combining my studies with night shifts covering racing, greyhounds and cricket. And from there I started getting interested in broadcasting, getting involved with a Rapid Raceline telephone line and Teamtalk service – all that sort of stuff.

**Where did you then start work after University?**
I started out working for Viking FM and Minster FM in York. Bizarrely my last ever shift on Viking FM was covering the Wolves' game at Grimsby on the first day of the 1996/97 season. And Bully got a hat trick! I could barely control myself to see my childhood hero banging in the goals when of course I was supposed to be covering

the game from a Grimsby perspective. It was due to be my last shift anyway but looking back I would probably have been sacked on the back of that commentary alone! From there I worked as a freelance for TalkSPORT which included covering world snooker.

**How did you first get involved with Sky?**
I found out Sky were recruiting for an Editorial Assistant for the Football League programme. I sent my CV in and had an interview which, to be honest, didn't go very well. I still managed to get a trial and ironically part of that was to interview Wolves strikers Ade Akinbiyi and Michael Branch at Molineux for the build-up to a live match with Birmingham. Again that didn't go massively well but I still managed to land the role, which is one up from being a 'runner'.

# Johnny Phillips

### And from there?
Basically I progressed through the ranks to become Assistant Producer and then Reporter. I made sure I put myself forward for anything and everything if other people were unavailable. I did as many interviews as I could and put a showreel together and went to see the Producer of Soccer Saturday. At the time there were no jobs available but it worked out well in the end because eventually an opportunity came up and I was delighted to take it on.

### Can you remember your first match assignment? The 'Kamara-Cam' as it has become known?
Yes it was at Sunderland for a game with Leicester towards the end of the season. I was massively nervous to be fair! And I remember I wore this horrendous red and white checked shirt. But once I got into it I really enjoyed it and the whole buzz of the programme was fantastic. Jeff Stelling had been urging them to give me a chance and I loved it. I think the feature interviews we do during the week feels more like normal work but the live stuff is just the big buzz of the job. Things can change so quickly and you have to be right at it to keep up.

### Is there a 'normal' week in terms of workload?
As a rule I'd say that each week we all cover two live games and have to produce two extensive features for Soccer Saturday. I got recognised in a pub in Liverpool once by a stag party (OR WAS IT HEN?) and they were all asking me what it is that we do for the rest of the week apart from two minutes on

a Saturday afternoon! Well there is always a lot to sort out with fixing up interviews, then there's the research and the travelling as well as the editing afterwards. It does get busy and there is never any time off during the season but it is also a privileged job to be doing when you are a football fan as well.

### Any particular stories to tell from your experience of Kamara-Cams?
There are a few! I always try and add something extra to the reporting by mentioning someone else if they are in shot such as a policeman or a steward. Sometimes people do try a bit too hard to get in the shot and I remember one slightly portly steward who kept going it so eventually I had to mention him. Then once I was stationed right next to the drummer at Blackpool so you can imagine how that one went! Other times people may shout out something dodgy or hold up a banner. You report from some fairly strange places and there was one ground where the gantry was very rickety and one of the Prozone analysts fell off and needed stitches! At Liverpool you have to climb through the rafters and walk down this corridor in the pitch black to get there. But it's all good fun!

### Any particular mistakes to remember?
I think my 'best' is probably when I interviewed Gareth Southgate when he was Middlesbrough captain. The cameraman wasn't ready so we had to spend a few minutes having some small talk. I asked Gareth if he'd watched the England/Holland game on telly the night before and I thought at the time he looked at me a bit funny. I made a joke of it but when he'd gone the cameraman asked if I'd meant to ask him that question. Turns out he'd actually played in the England match.......

### What's it like interviewing the managers after important games?

It's always said to reporters at Sky that the tunnels after matches are testosterone-fuelled areas with so much emotion and adrenalin swimming about. It can be very tricky to deal with certain situations and you have to try and keep calm but there can often be mishaps in interview environments. I remember Sir Alex Ferguson absolutely rinsing me after one bad question – it was a bad one so it was my fault.

### What are Jeff Stelling and the regular panellists like to work with?

They are great. Off-camera they are exactly like they are when you see them on the telly – really good fun. The banter is always flying around the office and Jeff is the ringmaster who handles

them brilliantly. They are all mad football fans as well, the same as everyone who watches the show. They are football experts who get predictions wrong and have opinions like all of us but overall are just massive football fans.

### Finally then, a Wolves fan with a Liverpool accent? How did that come about?

My Dad came over from Ireland in the mid-1950s and lived in London. His first game was at White Hart Lane when Wolves lost 4-3 to Tottenham. He loved the name and loved the kit so kept watching Wolves when they played in London – he was hooked! He moved to Liverpool where he met my Mum and when I was young I asked him to take me to Wolves and it went on from there!

### But of course you have to remain impartial?

Yes I do. It can be a labour of love doing interviews at Wolves and the players and indeed the club are great to deal with. But I always get my work head on and have to ask the difficult questions if needed. If I didn't I'd soon get found out. To be honest I find it very easy to be objective, particularly at matches. When we were in Liverpool and went to games like Wigan, Tranmere and Preston I was always in the home end so had to sit on my hands! So I find it easy to be neutral when I end up covering Wolves.

# Picture Perfect

It's not all about life on the pitch at a football club. Here the players are pictured involved in other activities such as charity and community events, many of which are run by the club's charity Wolves Community Trust or receive funding from Wolves Aid.

Sylvan Ebanks-Blake and several players paid a festive visit to Compton Hospice.

Adam Hammill shows off his tricks at one of the Wolves Soccer Schools.

olves Community Trust ambassador Matt Murray helped open Broadmeadow Special Community arsery School's sensory gymnasium and ball pool, Wolves Aid having helped with the fundraising.

Almost all of Wolves' 2003 promotion heroes returned to Molineux for a reunion dinner as part of Matt Murray's testimonial.

It was a successful year for the Kickz project run by Wolves Community Trust.

Karl Henry and Roger Johnson laid a wreath before the game with Aston Villa, in memory of the club's long-serving kitman Dave Plant.

Are you Rory McIlroy in disguise? Stephen Hunt chips out of a bunker at a golf day.

Players supported the promotion of the annual collection for Wolverhampton wheelchair charity Power Pleas.

Rachael Heyhoe-Flint and Matt Murray among those looking on as young fan Harry Cartwright sees the fruits of his labours to get a locomotive named after Wolverhampton Wanderers.

Wolves were keen supporters of the year's Sport Relief appeal.

Keepers Wayne Hennessey, Dorus De Vries and Aaron McCarey delivered a Wolves Aid grant for new play equipment at Cherry Trees School.

Kevin Foley was among the group of players spreading Christmas cheer in the Children's Ward at New Cross Hospital.

# DAVE EDWARDS

**DEBUT:** The last game of the 2002/03 season, for Shrewsbury against Scunthorpe. I was just 17, and came on as a sub. We lost 2-1.

**BEST MEMORY IN FOOTBALL:** Winning the Championship with Wolves.

**WORST MEMORY IN FOOTBALL:** Getting relegated.

**BEST GOAL:** My favourite is my first Wales goal, against Liechtenstein.

**BEST MATE IN FOOTBALL:** A few of the lads at Wolves such as Jarvo and Vokesey, and I'm still good mates with Joe Hart from our days at Shrewsbury.

**WHAT ADVICE WOULD YOU GIVE TO YOUNG PLAYERS?** Practice, practice, practice!

# AT THE DOUBLE!

The 2011/12 season was nothing less than an unqualified success for the Wolves Women team, as they were crowned Midland Combination League Champions to earn promotion.

This impressive achievement meant the ladies headed into the current campaign in the FA Women's Premier League Northern division, the third tier of Women's Football behind the Premier League National Division and – at the top – the Super League.

Wolves Women were beaten only once in their 20 league games, winning 14 and drawing five to win the title by two points from nearest challengers Stoke City Ladies.

The league title was sealed with a 4-1 away victory at Leafield Athletic on an evening kick off, Jamillah Palmer, Hannah Williams, Rebecca Large and Amber Quick grabbing the goals.

And the squad duly made it a double success by also beating Stoke in the final of the Midlands Combination League Cup, Jenny Anslow and Dani Selmes on target in a 2-0 win.

The victorious double winning squad then enjoyed a lap of honour at Molineux during half time of the final men's home game of the season with Everton.

# TEN REASONS TO CHEER!

Wolves Academy enjoyed another successful 2011/12 season both on and off the pitch, with a number of players graduating to first team honours, the club landing Category One status, and redevelopment plans getting into full swing. Here we look at ten reasons to be confident that the future is indeed gold!

## 1 ANTHONY FORDE

After a Carling Cup debut at Northampton, Anthony Forde's first three Barclays Premier League appearances came against Chelsea, Arsenal – and Chelsea again. Wow! The talented Irish midfielder, who joined the Academy at the age of 15, also enjoyed some action in the closing fixtures of the season.

## 2 DAVID DAVIS

Having developed his experience in several loan spells, David Davis didn't disappoint when recalled from League One duty with Chesterfield to the unforgiving Barclays Premier League. He quickly became a fans' favourite with some enterprising displays in the centre of midfield, confirming the potential shown when coming through the Academy.

## 3 THE REST....

There were plenty more moments to savour as well with full Northern Ireland international Johnny Gorman making a Premier League debut as a late substitute, and Jamie Reckord starting the Carling Cup tie with Northampton. A string of other Academy graduates also enjoyed impressive loan spells away from Molineux, headed by Danny Batth, a key figure in Sheffield Wednesday's promotion from League One. All are keen to follow in the footsteps of the likes of Wayne Hennessey, who has continued to excel having come through the ranks.

## 4 HOSPITAL VISIT

The off-field education and mentoring programme continues to ensure the Academy scholars become good people as well as good footballers! At Christmas, for the first time, the Academy scholars mirrored the community visits of the first team squad by visiting patients at Birmingham Children's Hospital. And, off their own initiative, the young players put in some of their earnings to buy presents to hand over to their children on the visit.

## 5 MAGNIFICENT SEVEN!

The Academy Under-18s enjoyed an impressive season in what was regarded as the toughest Premier League division. From October to December they won seven games in a row, scoring 20 goals against opponents including Manchester United, Manchester City, Everton and West Bromwich Albion.

## 6 REDEVELOPMENT

Part of the extensive Compton Park redevelopment, which will benefit the whole community and not just Wolves, will see a brand new single-site Academy facility meaning the operation no longer needs to be divided between Compton and Aldersley. The state-of-the-art new 3G pitch was constructed during the summer with the building developments to follow. Academy Manager Kevin Thelwell says the proposals will take Wolves' provision for young talent "to another level".

## 7 ACADEMY INTERNATIONALS

Several Academy scholars enjoyed more international experience at different levels over the season. Eyes down for Kristian Kostrna (Slovakia U21), Anthony Forde (Republic of Ireland U19), Liam McAlinden (Northern Ireland U19), Robbie Parry, Declan Weeks and Jordan Cranston (all Wales U19), Aljaz Cotman (Slovenia U19), Peter Smith (Wales U16), Ibrahim Keita (France U16), Ben O'Hanlon (England U16) and Cieron Keane (Republic of Ireland U16). Meanwhile three former Wolves Academy scholars no longer with the club – Joleon Lescott, Keith Andrews and Robbie Keane – appeared at the summer's European Championships.

## 8 EIGHT IS GREAT!

Wolves have no fewer than EIGHT players of the Academy intake who headed into the 2012/13 season with a professional contract. Anthony Forde, Zeli Ismail, Liam McAlinden, Aljaz Cotman and Kristian Kostrna already had their terms secured before the decisions to hand Jordan Cranston, Sam Whittall and Jake Kempton senior deals.

## 9 ZELI ON TOUR

Winger Zeli Ismail is hoping to continue his progress through the Academy ranks to one day succeed at senior level. But at the end of last season it was a trip-of-a-lifetime which captured his attention. Zeli was one of 16 young players from then Premier League clubs who visited townships in South Africa affected by poverty and carried out coaching sessions and worked with the local youngsters.

## 10 MAKING THE GRADE

Wolves received one of the coveted Category One statuses from the Premier League after an intensive and wide-ranging audit of the Academy's methods and facilities. This was awarded following the introduction of the Elite Player Performance Plan and, coupled with the redevelopment work, means Wolves will boast the best possible provision for the young players coming through the ranks.

# HENRY GOES BACK TO SCHOOL

Schooldays – the best days of your life right? The Wolves Annual thought they would put this to the test by quizzing one of our own – Molineux midfielder Karl Henry. Born in Wolverhampton, Karl was educated in his home city, at St Alban's Primary School in Ashmore Park and Coppice High School in Wednesfield. Here he digs into the memory bank to recall some of those happy times!

### FAVOURITE TEACHER?

At St Alban's it was Mrs Aldridge. She was really nice. Everyone loved her. She would set us targets and if you matched them and finished your work she would let you play! Me and my friend Gaz Llewellyn used to swop World Cup stickers and loads of football stuff. So we'd hit our targets in Mrs Aldridge's class and she'd let us do all that. At Coppice it was Mr Clifton. He was my PE teacher and took our football teams – he really loved his football. We managed to get to Wembley with the school team in Year Nine which was great. Although we ended up losing on penalties to Millwall before the play-off final between Leicester and Crystal Palace.

### FAVOURITE SUBJECT?

PE for obvious reasons. And Maths. I've always been quite good at Maths and have liked working with figures. In PE it wasn't just football. I used to love all sports. I was decent in tennis while in swimming I never lost a race in three years. That was either at the school or against other schools. I used to swim front crawl and breast stroke and never lost a race.

### WORST SUBJECT?

Religious Studies. However I have become more interested in the subject since I left. I used to have a lot of discussions about religion with David Jones. But in my school days I wasn't interested in learning about one religion. And while I wouldn't say I'm religious now, I am certainly intrigued.

### HOW DID YOU SPEND PLAY TIMES?

Football all the time! And a bit of kiss chase of course! There was a bit of that going on behind the bike sheds. Leanne Chilton and Laura Smith. Just little pecks on the cheek – primary school buddies, you know how it is. Then we'd play pitch and toss as well. And Three Card Brag. A lad called Andy Thompson came from London and taught us how to play Three Card Brag. In Year Seven I think. We'd gamble our lunch money on it!

### SCHOOL SIDELINES?

I was a bit of an entrepreneur at school. A wheeler-dealer. I mentioned in last year's Annual how I'd buy a pack of four Micro Chips for a pound, go home at break time to warm them up, and sell them individually for a pound each. 300 per cent profit. I also used to sell rubbers in primary school. I think my mate's mum worked somewhere and was able to buy a lot of rubbers cheaply with characters on them. So I started up a little business selling them at school.

### WAS KARL HENRY A GOOD STUDENT?

I think people think I was now! Ha ha! A few of my school reports make interesting reading. I remember one from my drama teacher. I didn't particularly like drama and they said I wouldn't listen. It was always "my way or the highway". Whenever we had to come up with something or do a scene I would dictate who was what. I just thought I was a captain in the making!

Karl with sister Latoya back in their schooldays.

Henry takes his place in his school photo at Coppice in 1994. (middle row third from left)

### DOES EDUCATION MATTER?

Looking back now I think I would say how education is really important. I was taken out of school halfway through my GCSE's when I moved to join Stoke. I only went to school three days a week then and the curriculums were different so some of the stuff I'd already learned never came up in the exams and there was loads of stuff on there I hadn't even studied. There were things about books on my exam papers I'd never even read but it wasn't because I hadn't applied myself – it was because I'd moved halfway through. I didn't think too much about it at the time because Stoke were so keen for me to play football and get up there early. Looking back I should have done more with my education and would certainly pass that advice on!

### ANYTHING MISSING IN EDUCATION?

I'd like to see kids taught finances at school. We never had it at our school and I don't think people have any idea what to do when they start earning money and what to do with it. I think kids should be told what sort of costs are involved in buying houses and cars and what kind of jobs they would need to do that. A more practical subject! I have been very fortunate in my job but I had no idea what I was doing with my money until I learned about it a few years into my career.

### STILL IN TOUCH WITH SCHOOL FRIENDS?

I'm still in touch with a few. One of the best men at my wedding was Simon Davis who was in the year below me at school. He still lives in Willenhall. I've been back to the schools a few times as well which is always nice. I'm also in touch with Lee Onions and Max Godridge from my schooldays, and Matt Johnson as well.

### BEST DAYS OF YOUR LIFE?

People say that because there are no responsibilities. Nobody explains what is to come afterwards either! You don't realise how lucky you are during your schooldays! They were really good times for me.

# KITMEN'S QUIZ

Wolves' dedicated duo of kitmen – Trev and Morts – are the members of the backroom staff charged with ensuring life runs smoothly on the kit and equipment front at both the Compton training ground and on matchdays both home and away.

As you can see from the picture, they combine this gainful employment with a rigorous fitness programme to ensure they remain in tip top shape – or maybe not. Moving on swiftly, we've got them together to provide a Kitmen's Quiz in this year's Annual. Using behind-the-scenes information which only they can know – well up until now anyway – they have set ten questions for fans to try and answer. Take it away gents.

1. **Before a match, who is always the last player out of the dressing room and doesn't put his shirt on until he comes out?**
   (a) Matt Jarvis
   (b) Stephen Hunt
   (c) Michael Kightly

2. **Which member of staff wears the most pieces of 'under-armour' below his kit?**
   (a) Tony Daley
   (b) Pat Mountain
   (c) Steve Kemp

3. **Which two players insist on having their own hats and gloves in the winter?**
   (a) Berra/Ebanks-Blake
   (b) Hunt/Doyle
   (c) Stearman/Ward

4. **Which player had the most pairs of boots during the 2011/12 season – a total of 17?**
   (a) Steven Fletcher
   (b) Matt Jarvis
   (c) Ronald Zubar

5. **Who spends the longest time in the shower?**
   (a) Karl Henry
   (b) Wayne Hennessey
   (c) Carl Ikeme

6. **Who is the only member of the squad to wear a headband?**
   (a) Richard Stearman
   (b) Stephen Hunt
   (c) Dave Edwards

7. **Who gives away the most shirts?**
   (a) Ronald Zubar
   (b) Kevin Foley
   (c) Karl Henry

8. **Who owns the most hair products?**
   (a) Stephen Hunt
   (b) Richard Stearman
   (c) Kevin Doyle

9. **Which member of the staff or squad wears kit a size too small for him to make him look bigger?**
   (a) Stephen Hunt
   (b) Tony Daley
   (c) Matt Jarvis

10. **Which player gives the kitmen the most verbal?**
    (a) Wayne Hennessey
    (b) Karl Henry
    (c) Stephen Ward

Answers on Page 61

# KEVIN FOLEY

**DEBUT:** Came off the bench for Luton as a 17-year-old in a Football League Trophy Game at Woking. We won 2-0.

**BEST MEMORY IN FOOTBALL:**
I've got a lot but probably the first time I was ever captain for Wolves, at Old Trafford against Manchester United, the team I supported as a boy.

**WORST MEMORY IN FOOTBALL:**
Two relegations, one with Luton and one with Wolves.

**BEST GOAL:** My first goal for Wolves against Norwich. I beat a couple of players and, unlike me; I rifled it into the bottom corner.

**BEST MATE IN FOOTBALL:**
Everyone is my friend in football!

**WHAT ADVICE WOULD YOU GIVE TO YOUNG PLAYERS?**
Nothing travels faster than the ball!

# TO BE FRANK

One of the new faces to arrive at Molineux this summer was young striker Frank Nouble. The Wolves Annual caught up with the 21-year-old to get to know him better via some quickfire questions. So here goes, let's get to Nou-ble him!

### First team you ever played for?
A team called the Red Lion, near where I lived in Lewisham in London. I started playing for them at maybe Under-8 level I think.

### First pair of boots?
They were Nike I think. I wanted the ones that the Brazilian striker Ronaldo wore. They're my favourite.

### First goal you ever scored?
For a club team it would have been Millwall at Under-10 level. It was against Chelsea, and I scored four in the game. That helped me get a move to Chelsea's Academy.

### And first senior goal?
That was on loan for Swansea against Watford. I came off the bench and scored fairly quickly to put us 3-0 up. It proved crucial as we won 3-2 in the end!

### Senior debut?
That was at Molineux strangely enough, for West Ham on the first day of the 2009/10 season when Wolves had just got back in the Premier League. I came on for Carlton Cole for the last two minutes and we won 2-0. I had to come on and track Andy Keogh back as I recall.

### Best goal scored?
The one I have enjoyed the most was for West Ham, away against Derby at Pride Park. We lost 2-1 but it was a rare start I had last season so I enjoyed scoring.

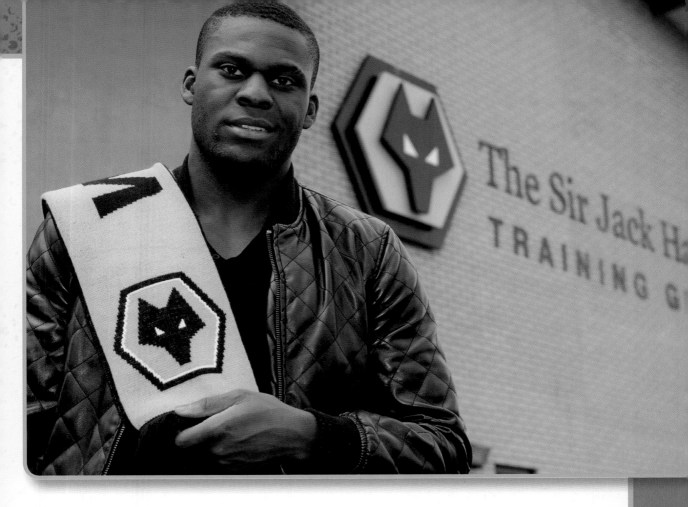

### Best moment of career so far?

I'd go back to that debut against Wolves in the Premier League. And also, when I was younger, playing for Chelsea in an FA Youth Cup game away at Manchester United. We won 3-2 at Old Trafford and I scored a really good goal in front of the Stretford End.

### Worst moment so far?

Touch wood I've not really had many really bad moments so far. Just any time I'm not playing I guess!

### Biggest influence on your career?

Didier Drogba. When I was at Chelsea he took an interest in me and followed what I was doing. He was a great role model for me to base my game on. He was easy to talk to and gave me lots of advice and was from the same country of origin – the Ivory Coast.

### Best advice ever had?

That was from Drogba. He just told me never to take any day for granted and just make the most of every training session or match. And always come off the pitch hurting!

### Best friend in football?

I've got a few. I'm good mates with Craig Eastmond who's at Arsenal, Sanchez Watt, and Nile Ranger.

### Finally, your career ambition?

To score as many goals as possible!

# WHO SAID IT?

So many words are spoken about Wolves over a season – but who came up with the quotes below during the 2011/12 campaign? Some are more easy to work out than others! It could be a Wolves player, member of the management staff or, in one case, one of the club's famous fans.

1. I don't feel like an injured player coming back from fitness anymore. I am keen to show people at Wolves – the management, players and the staff – that I'm back to how I used to be. I'm looking to try and get a good run of games and show people that I'm a Premier League player.

2. A long time ago I had a dream of playing or coaching in England. The playing side didn't last so long so hopefully the manager role lasts a lot longer! It's a new challenge for me and I have a good feeling in the stomach.

3. I've had five fantastic seasons here and am now going into my sixth. I'm still thoroughly enjoying it and to reach 200 appearances for Wolves is a good marker. It was a good way to celebrate my 200th with a good performance and a win against Fulham and now we move on to the next one!

4. We have tremendous ambition here. We wouldn't be spending the money on the stand, the Academy and on other things that we have done if we didn't have ambition.

5. It's not my game to make strong tackles or go in on people. I went into the challenge to take the ball and I got the ball first. I have never been sent off before – this was my first time.

6. I'll tell you how excited I was when Wolves went top of the Premier League. I've got a sports results 'app' on my phone, and I made sure I got a photo of the league table with Wolves at the top and have kept it as one of my pictures.

7. From the day I arrived I have settled at Wolves really well and everything has felt right. There have been setbacks along the way but it's also been a successful time and I think the club has always moved forward which is the most important thing.

8. I am looking forward to being put in the firing line – at least I think I am! Of course Matt is very well known for that memorable penalty save in the play-off final at the Millennium Stadium but now he's asked me to do this it's up to me to prove I can do exactly the same.

9. The fans were fantastic. It will be really raw for them and a tough period for them. But this is their club, and they must keep supporting their club. It is a really tough, emotional day for everyone and it will take a few days to come to terms with it.

10. I was really glad to score a goal like that. I often like to have a go and sometimes it goes in and sometimes it doesn't! I managed to control the ball well and push on to have a chance of the shot and when I hit it I thought it would go in.

# PUTTING THE BOOT IN

We've already enjoyed one quiz put together by Wolves' two kitmen Trev and Morts (see page 32). Well they don't know this but we raided the kit room again while they weren't looking. To grab 12 individual football boots belonging to the Wolves players. The tools of the job for all those who play football. Don't tell them will you?! Can you identify who these boots belong to? We've helped out with a clue or two along the way.

**1** This striker also has a couple of Golden versions of these.

**2** One of the more versatile members of the squad, this boot has been seen in various positions.

**3** This player covers plenty of ground in these every game, particularly making forward runs from midfield.

**4** The flag is a major hint for this player who was in action for his country at Euro 2012.

**5** Much is expected of this Wolves Academy graduate who broke into the first team in 2012.

**6** The left version of this scored one of the more crucial goals in Wolves' history.

**7** These boots can fly!

**8** Particularly used for tackling, this player once tripped over these.

**9** This keeper will always share the cost of a meal out.

**10** This player revels in shooting from distance.

**11** These boots are made for running – a long way. Regularly Wolves' biggest distance coverer in matches!

**12** "All we need is"....these boots to score a stunner against the local rivals.

Answers on Page 61

# BULLY'S BITES

Steve Bull loved playing for England in the 1990 World Cup in Italy so much that he opened an Italian restaurant 21 years later! Ok so the two are not directly connected, but Bravaccio's Italian restaurant offering a fine dining experience overlooking Tettenhall Green is proving another successful enterprise for the Wolves' legend. We caught up with the club's record goalscorer to run through some of the delights on offer on the Bravaccio's menu – and comparing some of their ingredients to his former team-mates! Hasta La Vista Bully!

### ZUPPA DEL GIORNI
Chef's Home Made Soup

**BULLY:** Soup is quite traditional and when it comes to traditional we had Lawrie Madden. Lawrie was old and traditional when he came to Wolves! He used to wear the same gear whatever the occasion – at home, abroad, anywhere. We called him Daktari because he always wore the same Khaki gear.

### CARPACCIO DI MANZO
Thinly sliced beef, served raw with a rocket, Parmesan and Caper berry salad and horseradish sauce to complement.

**BULLY:** Thin and gangly? Got to be Mike Stowell. He was a bit of a beanpole and always difficult to score against. He had the perfect name because he was certainly a Mickey-taker! But when he was on the pitch he got his blinkers on and did the business. He was a very good goalkeeper.

### COSTOLETTE DOLCE SPEZIA
Barbecued pork ribs seasoned with herbs and spices then generously smothered in a sweet chilli glaze.

**BULLY:** Ribs? Someone that always liked a dig in the ribs was Kevin Muscat! Muzzy never really meant to do it that hard but it was just how he was. Even I had to wince sometimes! But off the pitch he is great, a top man!

### EMILIA ROMAGNA
Classic Italian sharing platter consisting of prosciutto ham, Milano salami, Parma ham and Reggiano cheese with a rocket and olive salad.

**BULLY:** Sharing? I'd say in the 1980s we were all sharing and we were all tight – no one had any money! We were Fourth Division players. I think everyone just dug in together and whatever we had we shared. In that period the fact that everyone stuck together played a massive part in the team spirit and success that we enjoyed.

### CANNELLONI AL RICOTTA
Spinach and Ricotta cheese filled pasta rolls.

**BULLY:** Spinach builds up muscles and there were two team-mates I remember who liked to build up their muscles. Tony Daley and Cyrille Regis. Tony was ripped and was always in the gym pulling weights. Cyrille and me used to have different challenges – who could cycle the quickest, who could pull the most weights and so on.

### PENNE GORGONZOLA
Smooth creamy sauce with a strong cheese tang from the rich gorgonzola cheese.

**BULLY:** Cheesy. As in jokes. Got to be another keeper Mark Kendall, who is sadly no longer with us. He was the joker in the pack at that time, keeping the dressing room going by telling silly jokes or doing things to people's clothes. Some of the jokes weren't great – we used to laugh out of sympathy!

## SPAGHETTI BOLOGNESE

A traditional pasta dish that cannot be ignored for its simplicity and impeccable taste.

**BULLY:** I daren't call Thommo simple but he has impeccable taste – he's mates with me! We signed on the same day and he was my room-mate. He's a bossy little bugger but I love him to bits and we would always stick up for each other at Wolves.

## IL BRAVACCIO

Our house special beef burger with hand torn mozzarella pieces infused into the burger. Served on a toasted ciabatta with our chef's own famous thick-cut chips and a rocket and beef tomato garnish.

**BULLY:** Our burgers are great but back in the day I was the one who went for the McDonalds option. And after training I'd go off to the Goalpost for sausage, egg, chips and beans and then sometimes McDonalds for tea. I don't think it ever did me any harm!

## VITELLO MARSALA

Prime escalope of veal cooked in a marsala wine sauce with roasted seasonal vegetables and our herby new potatoes.

**BULLY:** Veal is of course a baby cow, and there were a few baby-faced apprentices coming through when I was playing – Lee Naylor, Keith Andrews, Joleon Lescott, Matt Murray. Matt used to try and cheek me a bit to be honest. So I had to give him a bit of a squeeze or a headlock to put him in his place. No problem!

## POLLO AL RISOTTO

A supreme breast of locally sourced chicken pan-fried in a light garlic oil served with creamy risotto, finished with a balsamic reduction.

**BULLY:** There weren't many 'chickens' around in our day! Maybe I'll go for Tim Steele on the wing. He'd moan even when it was hardly a tackle. The opposite would be Keith Downing. He was a hard man in training or games, a Jack Russell in getting about the pitch. But that was the way he played and everyone respected that and would always get up and shake hands after.

## FILETTO LA GRIGLIA

28-day hung and aged fillet steak served with the chef's famous thick-cut chips, a whole field mushroom and roasted vine tomatoes.

**BULLY:** Steak and chips – what a great combination. And myself and Andy Mutch had a great relationship on the pitch and he was the best strike partner I had. He's a Scouser and never shuts up and while we couldn't understand each other's accents we always knew where we were on the pitch.

## BRAVACCIO AL IMPAURITO

Swapping the mince beef for a thick baked field mushroom with melted mozzarella on a ciabatta bun with beef tomato slices and a rocket side.

**BULLY:** When you talk about 'rockets' then Robbie Dennison was someone who could shoot from distance and take a great free kick. Denno was a really tricky winger and I think one of the best wingers Wolves have had recently. He's a great fella off the pitch as well – spot on.

## SALMONE ALLA ROMAGNA

Seared salmon steak cooked in a double cream and white wine sauce, served with herby new potatoes and seasonal vegetables.

**BULLY:** White wine, that wasn't really for us as players. We were lager louts! Only joking! The gaffer Graham Turner would be the man you'd find having a quiet glass of white wine when we were away.

Bravaccio's can be found overlooking the green at Tettenhall five minutes from Wolverhampton City Centre. Phone (01902) 756052 or visit www.bravaccios.co.uk for more details and to view the full menu.

# Player Profiles

Here are the profiles for the most senior members of the Wolves squad who contributed to the team during the 2011/12 season.

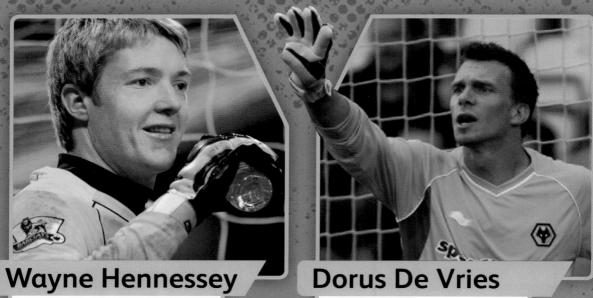

## Wayne Hennessey

**POSITION:** GOALKEEPER
**BORN:** 24/01/87
**NICKNAME:** HENNO
**APPS:** 34
**GOALS:** 0

## Dorus De Vries

**POSITION:** GOALKEEPER
**BORN:** 29/12/80
**NICKNAME:** GRANDAD
**APPS:** 9
**GOALS:** 0

## Carl Ikeme

**POSITION:** GOALKEEPER
**BORN:** 08/06/86
**NICKNAME:** KEEMS
**APPS:** 0 (1)
**GOALS:** 0

## Kevin Foley

**POSITION:** DEFENDER
**BORN:** 01/11/84
**NICKNAME:** FOLES/FOJAM
**APPS:** 12 (6)
**GOALS:** 0

Appearances and goals shown are in all competitions with additional substitute appearances in brackets.

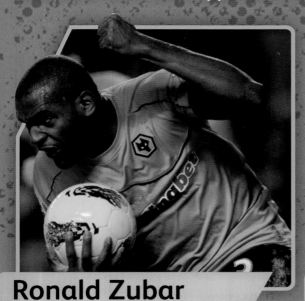

## Ronald Zubar

**POSITION:** DEFENDER
**BORN:** 20/09/85
**NICKNAME:** ZUBEY
**APPS:** 14 (1)
**GOALS:** 1

## Richard Stearman

**POSITION:** DEFENDER
**BORN:** 19/08/87
**NICKNAME:** STEARS/STERNZY
**APPS:** 31 (2)
**GOALS:** 0

## Matt Doherty

**POSITION:** DEFENDER
**BORN:** 16/01/92
**NICKNAME:** DOC
**APPS:** 4 (1)
**GOALS:** 0

## Stephen Ward

**POSITION:** DEFENDER
**BORN:** 20/08/85
**NICKNAME:** WARDY
**APPS:** 40 (1)
**GOALS:** 3

## George Elokobi

**POSITION:** DEFENDER
**BORN:** 31/01/86
**NICKNAME:** KOBES
**APPS:** 8 (6)
**GOALS:** 1

## Christophe Berra

**POSITION:** DEFENDER
**BORN:** 31/01/85
**NICKNAME:** BERRA!
**APPS:** 32 (3)
**GOALS:** 0

## Roger Johnson

**POSITION:** DEFENDER
**BORN:** 28/04/83
**NICKNAME:** RODGE
**APPS:** 27 (1)
**GOALS:** 0

## Jody Craddock

**POSITION:** DEFENDER
**BORN:** 25/07/75
**NICKNAME:** JODE
**APPS:** 3
**GOALS:** 0

## Sebastien Bassong

LOAN

**POSITION:** DEFENDER
**BORN:** 09/07/86
**NICKNAME:** BAS
**APPS:** 9
**GOALS:** 0

## Karl Henry

**POSITION:** MIDFIELD
**BORN:** 26/11/82
**NICKNAME:** HENRYAMA
**APPS:** 31 (2)
**GOALS:** 0

## David Davis

**POSITION:** MIDFIELD
**BORN:** 20/02/91
**NICKNAME:** DD
**APPS:** 6 (2)
**GOALS:** 0

## Eggert Jonsson

**POSITION:** MIDFIELD
**BORN:** 18/08/88
**NICKNAME:** EGGERT
**APPS:** 4 (1)
**GOALS:** 0

# Player Profiles

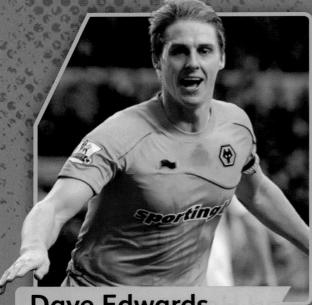

## Dave Edwards

**POSITION:** MIDFIELD
**BORN:** 03/02/86
**NICKNAME:** EDDO
**APPS:** 28 (2)
**GOALS:** 4

## Jamie O'Hara

**POSITION:** MIDFIELD
**BORN:** 25/09/86
**NICKNAME:** J
**APPS:** 19 (1)
**GOALS:** 3

## Adlene Guedioura

**POSITION:** MIDFIELD
**BORN:** 12/11/85
**NICKNAME:** ADDY
**APPS:** 4 (9)
**GOALS:** 1

## Nenad Milijaš

**POSITION:** MIDFIELD
**BORN:** 30/04/83
**NICKNAME:** NED
**APPS:** 10 (14)
**GOALS:** 2

## Anthony Forde

**POSITION:** MIDFIELD
**BORN:** 16/11/93
**NICKNAME:** FORDEY
**APPS:** 3 (4)
**GOALS:** 0

LOAN

## Emmanuel Frimpong

**POSITION:** MIDFIELD
**BORN:** 10/01/92
**NICKNAME:** MANNY/DENCH
**APPS:** 5
**GOALS:** 0

## Michael Kightly

**POSITION:** WINGER
**BORN:** 24/01/86
**NICKNAME:** KIGHTS
**APPS:** 16 (5)
**GOALS:** 3

## Adam Hammill

**POSITION:** WINGER
**BORN:** 25/01/88
**NICKNAME:** LAR
**APPS:** 6 (7)
**GOALS:** 1

## Stephen Hunt

**POSITION:** WINGER
**BORN:** 01/08/81
**NICKNAME:** HUNTY/FRODO
**APPS:** 19 (9)
**GOALS:** 3

## Matt Jarvis

**POSITION:** WINGER
**BORN:** 22/05/86
**NICKNAME:** JARVO
**APPS:** 31 (8)
**GOALS:** 8

## Sam Vokes

**POSITION:** STRIKER
**BORN:** 21/10/89
**NICKNAME:** TOSH
**APPS:** 3 (5)
**GOALS:** 2

## Sylvan Ebanks-Blake

**POSITION:** STRIKER
**BORN:** 29/03/86
**NICKNAME:** SYLV
**APPS:** 11 (15)
**GOALS:** 3

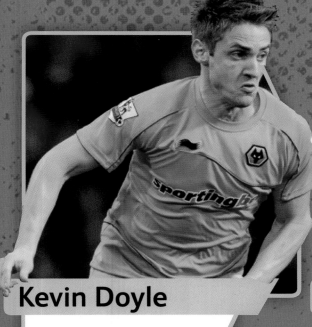

## Kevin Doyle

**POSITION:** STRIKER
**BORN:** 18/09/83
**NICKNAME:** DOYLER
**APPS:** 30 (6)
**GOALS:** 4

## Steven Fletcher

**POSITION:** STRIKER
**BORN:** 26/03/87
**NICKNAME:** FLETCH
**APPS:** 26 (8)
**GOALS:** 12

The remaining members of the squad shown below were either senior players who spent last season on loan elsewhere or the club's younger or newly-signed professionals.

### Steven Mouyokolo
**DEFENDER**

### Danny Batth
**DEFENDER**

### Jamie Reckord
**DEFENDER**

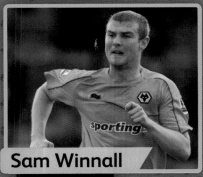

### Sam Winnall
**STRIKER**

### Johnny Gorman
**WINGER**

### Nathaniel Mendez-Laing
**WINGER**

# Player Profiles

**Leigh Griffiths**

STRIKER

**Jake Cassidy**

STRIKER

**Kristian Kostrna**

DEFENDER

**Jake Kempton**

STRIKER

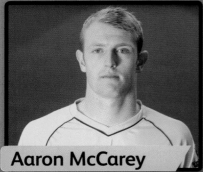

**Aaron McCarey**

GOALKEEPER

**Ethan Ebanks-Landell**

DEFENDER

**Jordan Cranston**

DEFENDER

**Aljaz Cotman**

GOALKEEPER

**Jack Price**

MIDFIELDER

**Michael Ihiekwe**

DEFENDER

**Sam Whittall**

MIDFIELDER

**Zeli Ismail**

WINGER

**Liam McAlinden**

STRIKER

48

# RICHARD STEARMAN

**DEBUT:** It was for Leicester in a 0-0 draw away at Cardiff. I came off the bench as a 17-year-old in the closing stages to play in the centre of midfield.

**BEST MEMORY IN FOOTBALL:** Getting promoted with Wolves.

**WORST MEMORY IN FOOTBALL:** Getting relegated with Wolves.

**BEST GOAL:** Scoring with a bicycle kick for Leicester against Sheffield Wednesday.

**BEST MATE IN FOOTBALL:** I've got a fair few – mainly Fletch, Kights and Wardy at Wolves.

**WHAT ADVICE WOULD YOU GIVE TO YOUNG PLAYERS?** Give your best whether in training or matches – someone is always watching.

# SYLVAN'S TOP TEN GOALS

Wolves sharp-shooter Sylvan Ebanks-Blake has been among the goals from the day he arrived at Molineux back in January, 2008.

Twice the winner of the Championship's Golden Boot, Sylvan also has a fair collection of top quality strikes among his varied assortment of goals.

We asked him to pick out ten of his best, not only for their quality but also their significance.

Here, in chronological order, is Sylvan's top ten.

### FIRST SENIOR GOAL (26/10/05)

Picture above: It was a Carling Cup game with Barnet that was my full debut for Manchester United. And I left it late, with one minute to go! I remember it quite well. There was a bit of a scramble in the box and I came away with it and tucked it in with my left foot. I was delighted to get a goal in my first start.

### FIRST GOAL FOR WOLVES (19/01/08)

This one was against Scunthorpe. I ran onto a pass and was one-on-one with the keeper and managed to dink it over him. Again it's always good to get off the mark early at a new club and I think that was my second game.

### BEST EVER (29/03/08)

My goal at Charlton was certainly my best ever. I can't say I'd ever tried the trick before that got me past the defender – it was just instinct! It was just nice to finish it off afterwards. And all of it on my birthday as well! Happy days.

Picture : John Peters/Manchester United FC.

## BACK AT OLD TRAFFORD (6/11/10)

Picture above: It was good to get another goal at Old Trafford, and this time for Wolves. I'd just come on a couple of minutes earlier and after Nenad's shot dropped to me I managed to score with my left foot. It was an equaliser and it was just a shame we went on to lose the game in the last minute of injury time. But it was definitely a nice moment for me personally.

## ON THE OVERHEAD! (27/09/08)

A different goal this one against Bristol City at home. I had my back to goal and was slipping as I struck the ball but I managed to get an overhead kick which went in. It was a good finish and we had a good day as a team that one.

## SNOW JOKE! (28/10/08)

It was a really cold night against Swansea at Molineux and there was still a bit of snow on the pitch. I managed to get the ball under control and get into the box and slot it past the keeper. It was quite a different goal for me on a tricky surface and is certainly one of my favourites.

## HAT TRICK KING (03/02/09)

Picture left: My only hat trick so far has been against Norwich and so the third goal to clinch it was special. I've got a good record against Norwich and was delighted to get a hat trick. If I remember I think I controlled the ball and fired through a packed goalmouth.

## SUPERSUB! (27/11/10)

Picture above: Another late one and a winning goal against Sunderland at Molineux. I'd come off the bench and Hunty had equalised to make it 2-2. Doyler played it in to me well and I think the keeper tried to guess where I was going. I took a bit of time and then smashed it and it ended up a good finish.

## PROMOTION CLINCHER (16/04/09)

Picture far left: The goal which took us into the Premier League. It was a great pullback from Andy Keogh and I just slotted in. Destiny! That was a great day for all of us.

## TWO TOUCH AND IN (28/10/10)

Picture right: I really liked that goal against Newcastle. Jelle Van Damme crossed and it sort of came over my head but with two touches it was in the back of the net. I was really pleased with how I managed to bring it down and I pride myself on those sorts of finishes in the box.

# WOLFIE WORKS OUT

Mascot Wolfie is not just one super-doopa furry growling machine seen on match days and supporting club events. He's also a pretty mean mover on the dance floor. So we dragged him from his lair to show off some of his steps pitchside – complete with choreography – to Michael Jackson's Thriller!

WELL HELLO WOLFIE. FANCY SEEING YOU HERE!

HERE HE GOES! HEAD DOWN UNTIL THE MUSIC STARTS AND THEN SNAP YOUR HEAD UP AND HOLD FOR A COUNT OF THREE!

TWITCH YOUR LEFT SHOULDER AND YOUR HEAD FOR EIGHT COUNTS AND THEN REPEAT WITH RIGHT.

ARMS OUT IN FRONT OF YOU AND BEHIND AND STEP YOUR FRONT FOOT FORWARD AND THEN YOUR BACK FOOT.

STEP FORWARD WITH YOUR RIGHT FOOT AND WAVE YOUR HANDS IN A LOW CIRCLE 'THE HIP FLOWER' – SWAP TO THE LEFT FOOT AND DO IT AGAIN.

FEET TOGETHER. HEAD FORWARD AND JERK AROUND LIKE A ZOMBIE FOR EIGHT QUICK COUNTS.

There's also a very serious side to Wolfie's exercise with Wolves Community Trust currently involved in a three-year 'Wolfie's Workouts' project. The physical activity initiative is a workout offered to all Primary Schools based in Wolverhampton, involving eight activities suitable for children and including a motivational DVD featuring Wolfie and a number of professional athletes. For further information please contact Wolves Community Trust on (01902) 828385.

JUMP UP AND FACE THE LEFT AND THRUST YOUR HIPS FORWARD FOR FOUR COUNTS BEFORE DOING SAME TO THE RIGHT.

FACE FORWARD. POINT HANDS DOWN AND SHAKE ARMS WITH A LITTLE SHIMMY...

...BEFORE CLAPPING TWICE OVER LEFT SHOULDER. REPEAT TO THE RIGHT!

HANDS ON HIPS. STEP AROUND IN A SEMI CIRCLE FOR SIX COUNTS AND THEN...

...LOOK BACK AT AUDIENCE BEFORE DOING SIX STEPS FORWARD.

SHIMMY HIPS TO THE LEFT FOR THREE COUNTS. LEFT HAND IN THE AIR. AND THEN SAME TO THE RIGHT.

HANDS UP IN A 'CLAW'. THREE STOMPS TO THE LEFT AND SWING ARMS TO THE RIGHT. SWING THEM AROUND SOME MORE!

THREE STOMPS FORWARD AND THEN DROP YOUR HEAD DOWN. YOU'RE DONE. A THRILLER!

TAKE A BOW SON!

# WAYNE'S WORLD OF RACING

Wayne with Yensi, one of his winners.

The Hennessey family after Marksbury comes home at Wolverhampton.

Wayne Hennessey was Wolves' Player of the Year for the 2011/12 season, the Welsh international keeping his standards consistently high despite the team's struggles. But not only is Wayne good at keeping goal, he's also showing plenty of promise in his off-pitch hobby – keeping horses! Wayne Hennessey the horse owner reveals more about his big passion away from football.

## MY RACING INTEREST

It started through my Dad Paul. He has always liked the horses. I remember when I was a little boy he took me to the Races at Carlisle and I loved it. It runs through the family, the male side anyway! I used to go a lot to Wolverhampton Races at Dunstall even before I owned a horse because obviously it was local to me. And the people at the racecourse have been brilliant with their support of me, with being my shirt sponsor and all that.

## MY FIRST HORSE

The first horse that I owned was called Heredias. Unfortunately though he died, the night after we beat Liverpool at Anfield a couple of seasons ago. I was on a real high after that game but then I got a call from my Dad telling me he'd been called out to the stables. The vet said he was in pain and needed to be put down so it happened while I was on the pitch. It quickly went from one of my best days to one of my worst.

Marksbury crosses the line in the race in memory of Wayne's Grandad.

The first ever winner – Oscar Close.

## MY FIRST WINNER

My first winner was a horse called Oscar Close. It won at Leicester two years ago and I was there to see it along with my family. It was fantastic, an incredible feeling which is impossible to describe. I imagine at a bigger race it would be even more incredible but to see your own horse cross the line first is brilliant. It's something you can't actually affect so it's so different to playing football. As of now I've had six winners , and each and every one of them have been special.

## A FAMILY AFFAIR

Horseracing is a real family thing for me. We all go to the races, have a nice meal and then cheer on my horse if it's running. Towards the end of the last football season we sponsored a race at Wolverhampton in memory of my Grandad. It would have been his birthday on the day of the race. And my horse Marksbury actually won! I think my Grandad was on the back of him that day, pushing him along!

## FOOTBALLERS' HOBBY

A lot of footballers are into the horses and you see a lot of them at race meetings. And it's not really for the betting. Like me a lot of others just love the sport particularly if you're fortunate enough to be able to own a horse. It's a great release to relax and take your mind off football. Having said that, if one of my horses is running I'm sometimes more nervous than when I'm playing!

## MY HORSERACING FUTURE

I've got six horses in total now including some at Kinsale Stud which isn't too far from Shrewsbury. Two race on the flat, one over the jumps and the others are broodmares. I do want to be a breeder eventually. But like all owners, to get a runner at Cheltenham or Ascot would be great as well!

# PREMIER FAMOUS FIVE

Relegation in the 2011/12 season made it a disappointing end to Wolves' three year stint in the Barclays Premier League, but amid the difficult times there were also plenty of thrills and spills to savour. Most notably the victories against some of the top teams in the country, and also Europe. Time therefore to re-live five of the glorious Wolves performances which toppled the big boys. And remember – we will be back!

## 1 DECEMBER 12, 2009: SPURS 0-1 WOLVES

An early Kevin Doyle flicked header from Nenad Milijas's free kick put Wolves in front against a Spurs side who had stuck nine past Wigan in their previous home game. But Wolves proved themselves to be made of stern stuff as they hung on to their lead for 87 minutes of normal time and an additional six added on.

### They Said:

> We defended brilliantly.
> At times we played well,
> but we had to put so much work
> in to get that result.
> It wasn't easy.
>
> *Kevin Doyle*

## 2 OCTOBER 30, 2010: WOLVES 2-1 MANCHESTER CITY

Wolves finally turned the promise of some decent performances against the big teams into a victory by coming from behind to defeat big-spending Manchester City. Emmanuel Adebayor's penalty put City in front but Nenad Milijas equalised and Dave Edwards fired past good friend Joe Hart to grab the 57th minute winner.

### They Said:

> I was with Joe at
> Shrewsbury and he rented a room
> off me for peanuts at the time –
> when the ball came back to me
> I couldn't really miss.
>
> *Dave Edwards*

### 3 DECEMBER 29, 2010: LIVERPOOL 0-1 WOLVES

A first win at Anfield for almost 27 years was sealed thanks to Stephen Ward's first goal in almost four years on a magical Christmas night in Liverpool. Ward, controversially sent off on the same ground a year previously, converted Sylvan Ebanks-Blake's precision pass on 56 minutes as Wolves also registered their first away win of the 2010/11 campaign.

## They Said:

*" To get a goal at Anfield is brilliant and I'm delighted – it's probably the most important moment of my career. "*

*Stephen Ward*

### 4 JANUARY 5, 2011: WOLVES 1-0 CHELSEA

Another wonderful Wolves Wednesday came seven days later after victory at Anfield, as reigning champions Chelsea were despatched at Molineux. The fifth minute breakthrough was scrappy as Jose Bosingwa diverted Stephen Hunt's corner into his own net but no one really cared as an excellent defensive display secured another vital three points.

## They Said:

*" It was terrific and we are all delighted, relieved, shattered as you can imagine. "*

*Mick McCarthy*

### 5 FEBRUARY 5, 2011: WOLVES 2-1 MANCHESTER UNITED

Wolves were bottom, and unbeaten Manchester United were top, and Wolves had suffered a devastating injury time loss at Bolton three days earlier.
But goals from George Elokobi and Kevin Doyle overhauled Nani's early opener prompting another famous Molineux night and saw Wolves became the first team in ten months and 30 attempts to beat United in the league.

## They Said:

*" Sir Alex called me a lucky so-and-so but he said it with his tongue in his cheek and a smile on his face and said we'd earned it. "*

*Mick McCarthy*

# KARAOKE KINGS

It's now a time-honoured Wolves tradition that when a player travels to an away game for the first time they have to stand up after dinner – in front of the whole squad – and sing a song of their selection! Many have said it's a more nerve-wracking experience than actually playing in the match the following day! Anyway, we collared a few of the players to ask what would be their chosen ditty to become Karaoke Kings. Drum roll please......

**NATHANIEL MENDEZ-LAING**
Say What's Real – Drake

**JOHNNY GORMAN**
Fit But You Know It – The Streets

**DAVE EDWARDS**
Don't Look Back In Anger – Oasis

**STEPHEN HUNT**
Ireland's Call (Rugby Song) – Phil Coulter

**DAVID DAVIS**
Headlines – Drake

**DORUS DE VRIES**
Stand By Me –
Ben E King

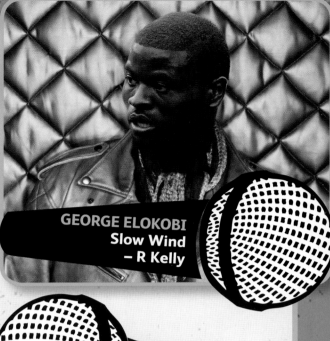

**GEORGE ELOKOBI**
Slow Wind
– R Kelly

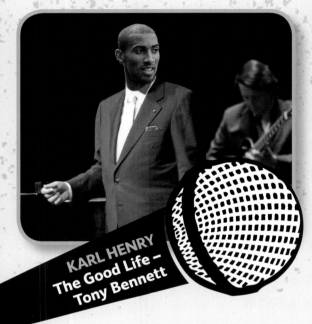

**KARL HENRY**
The Good Life –
Tony Bennett

**AARON MCCAREY**
Seven Drunken Nights
– The Dubliners

**JAMIE O'HARA**
The Gambler –
Kenny Rogers

**CARL IKEME**
What's Going On
– Marvin Gaye

**CHRISTOPHE BERRA**
Flower of Scotland – Roy
Williamson

**STEPHEN WARD AND
ANTHONY FORDE**
Galway Girl – Steve Earle/
Sharon Shannon

# IRISH EYES ARE SMILING

Wolves once again spent a week of pre-season in Ireland and, away from the football, there was time for some relaxation. Here are a few snapshots from Carton House Hotel, with the odd funny caption thrown in!

Karl Henry, ahem, enjoys a post-training ice bath.

"I knew I could have won some England caps in cricket...."

Steady on Foles – if the wind changes it will stick.

"I wonder when everyone will realise my hand is stuck to this golf ball."

Nenad quietly celebrates a Pro Evo victory.

Roger's camoflauge outfit works a treat on the golf course.

"Oh boss they didn't tell me how bad your jokes are!"

"If I laugh long enough will they ignore the fact there's no water in here?"

## WORDSEARCH (Page 20)

| B | N | N | U | T | S | O | P | L | A | O | G | O | L | A |
|---|---|---|---|---|---|---|---|---|---|---|---|---|---|---|
| W | A | I | Y | U | S | U | B | S | T | I | T | U | T | E |
| O | P | L | E | R | C | C | G | O | C | A | L | P | O | R |
| L | L | I | L | B | A | D | A | T | O | C | S | A | M | E |
| F | E | A | L | W | R | E | F | E | R | E | E | L | A | F |
| Q | N | M | O | A | F | C | O | R | N | E | F | E | N | F |
| R | N | Z | W | H | I | S | T | L | E | E | F | X | A | W |
| O | U | E | C | A | R | I | V | A | R | S | T | A | G | H |
| S | T | J | A | C | K | F | W | B | F | M | T | K | E | I |
| S | T | W | R | L | A | E | I | F | L | O | W | A | R | T |
| I | J | A | D | O | T | O | C | S | A | R | L | T | N | S |
| T | U | R | N | S | T | I | L | E | G | B | U | S | D | D |

## OLD HABITS DIE HARD! (Page 20)

1. Sylvan Ebanks-Blake
2. Adam Hammill
3. Dave Edwards
4. George Elokobi
5. Stephen Ward
6. Richard Stearman
7. Karl Henry
8. Kevin Foley
9. Stephen Hunt
10. Dorus De Vries

## KITMEN'S QUIZ (page 32)

1. (a)  2 (b)  3 (a)  4 (c)  5 (a)
6 (b)  7 (a)  8 (b)  9 (b)  10 (a)

## PUTTING THE BOOT IN (page 37)

1. Sylvan Ebanks-Blake
2. Kevin Foley
3. Dave Edwards
4. Stephen Ward
5. David Davis
6. Stephen Hunt
7. Michael Kightly
8. Richard Stearman
9. Dorus De Vries
10. Adlene Guedioura
11. Karl Henry
12. Jamie O'Hara

## WHO SAID IT? (page 36)

1. Michael Kightly
2. Ståle Solbakken
3. Karl Henry
4. Steve Morgan
5. Nenad Milijaš
6. Beverley Knight
7. Kevin Doyle
8. Jez Moxey
9. Terry Connor
10. Adlene Guedioura

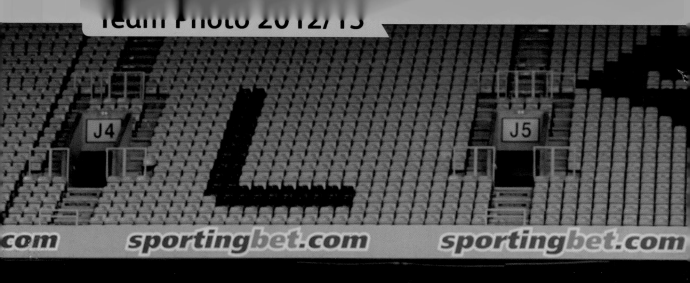